This Book Belongs To:

ISBN 13: 978-1-4621-4737-3

Published by CFI, an imprint of Cedar Fort, Inc.
2373 W. 700 S., Suite 100, Springville, UT 84663
Distributed by Cedar Fort, Inc., www.cedarfort.com

Cover design by Jenna Conlin and Shawnda T. Craig
Cover design © 2024 Cedar Fort, Inc.
Edited by Sarina Betts
Typeset by Sarina Betts and Shawnda T. Craig
Printed in the United States of America

10 9 8 7 6 5 4 3 2 1

Printed on acid-free paper

True Identity

Understanding Your Divine Destiny

A 6-Week Guide

Seeking Diligently

CFI
An imprint of Cedar Fort, Inc.
Springville, Utah

Contents

A Letter to You vii

Meet the Author, Rachel Rhien Tucker.....................viii

Meet the Artist, Angela Smith ix

Week One - Your Divine Identity.................................1

Week Two - Your Divine Worth.................................13

Week Three - Your Divine Agency 25

Week Four - Your Divine Gifts 35

Week Five - Your Divine Potential 45

Week Six - Your Divine Destiny 55

Reflect and Review 66

References 68

A Letter to You

2020 was a year of much learning. It was, for many, a year of trials and disappointments, heartache and loneliness. We all made changes. We each adapted to a "new normal." Part of that "new normal" for me was an early morning routine that consisted of meaningful personal prayer, meditation, affirmations, a gratitude journal, scripture study, and exercise.

I was already used to getting up early from the five years I spent as an early-morning seminary teacher, and I quickly found that this time, when it's quiet and I'm alone, is when I can most easily "hear Him." My journaling took on new depth; I reshaped my scripture study from simply reading and marking to studying specific topics; I strengthened my meditation muscles and learned to affirm myself; I received personal, unique revelation from heaven and recorded those things for the future.

One of the undeniable impressions I received was that I needed to use my love of learning, my gift of teaching, my ability to write, and my experiences teaching seminary to create a series of topical, doctrinal study guides for women young and old. It felt like a mission call. Thoughts came pouring into my mind. Beautiful talks and speeches started to surface. The scriptures took on a new meaning to me. I wanted to start this series of guides with an in-depth study of the divinity within each of us.

As a mother of four, I have a deep desire to teach my children about their divine heritage. I want them to internalize not only the fact that they are each children of God, but that they are known and loved by heavenly parents who want them to succeed. I want them to know that they are unique and that they've each been blessed with spiritual gifts that will help them on their journey. I hope that they will realize their potential and the blessings that can be theirs if they remember these truths and keep their minds and hearts focused on the Savior.

My hope is the same for you. As you come to understand more clearly your divine origin, I pray that you will strengthen your relationship with your Heavenly Father and that your divine identity and unique gifts lead you to believe more deeply in yourself, bless the lives of those around you, and live up to the inherent privileges that are yours.

Rachel

Meet the Author

Rachel Rhien Tucker is a wife and mother of four who lives in Southern California. Rachel graduated from Northern Arizona University and earned a bachelor's degree in Spanish. She has lived in a number of different countries and continues to value the education that comes with travel. Rachel is the owner and CEO of Seeking Diligently, where she is a writer and public speaker. Rachel has spoken at many women's conferences and hosted her own gathering, Arise Conference, in 2023. She is excited about the prospect of expanding that conference to new areas.

Rachel is most in her element when teaching or writing about the gospel of Jesus Christ. She taught early-morning seminary for five years and loves teaching others how to apply the scriptures to their lives. Rachel writes a daily devotional on Instagram and can be found @seeking_diligently.

Meet the Artist

Jenna Conlin was raised in Tucson, Arizona, by creative and hardworking parents who always supported her artistic growth. She was further encouraged by a wonderful set of public school art teachers and continued on to Brigham Young University's illustration program, taking many of the Art Department's more conceptual courses as well.

Jenna found that creating her own religious art aided her spiritual progression and helped her connect with those around her. In her final year at BYU, she interned for J. Kirk Richards, a prominent artist in the Church community. This experience encouraged her to continue pursuing her aspirations as a religious painter.

Jenna spends most of her time painting but also enjoys long-distance running, reading, and spending time with her husband.

Jenna's art focuses on what it feels like to be a modern-day disciple of Jesus Christ. She is interested in where realism meets abstraction and feels that she can communicate spiritual matters most cohesively in this space. Because her work grows from her own experience, it often has feminine themes. She hopes that people will connect with her art and is grateful for the connection it provides her to her heavenly parents.

Genesis 1:27 – So God created man in *his own image*, in the *image of God* created he him; male and female created he them.

Week One

Your Divine Identity

You are the spirit child of heavenly parents who love you. You were created to be uniquely individual. You are like them—in both body and spirit. You have a divine nature which makes it possible to communicate with and become like them. You are a phenomenal and important part of God's plan, and He trusts you to be His hands here on the earth. You are the literal spirit sibling of Jesus Christ. He loves you, and He made a way for you to be able to return to your heavenly family.

President Dieter F. Uchtdorf said, "Much of the confusion we experience in this life comes from simply not understanding who we are. Too many go about their lives thinking they are of little worth when, in reality, they are elegant and eternal creatures of infinite value with potential beyond imagination. Discovering who we really are is part of this great adventure called life. God has given again in these latter days the truths about where we came from, why we are here, and where we are going. You are something divine— more beautiful and glorious than you can possibly imagine. This knowledge changes everything. It changes your present. It can change your future. And it can change the world" ("The Reflection in the Water").

Memorization Scripture:

Psalm 82:6

"I have said, Ye are gods; and all of you are children of the most High."

Personal Affirmation:

As a literal child of God, I have a divine nature and identity. I seek to honor the divinity within me by communing with my Heavenly Father each day and living up to the sacred privileges that are mine.

Your Divine Identity

DAILY READING:

"Children of Heavenly Father," by M. Russell Ballard
BYU Speeches March 2020

Romans 8:16–18 • Matthew 5:14, 16

Q: Romans 8:16 talks about knowing who we are through the whisperings of the Spirit. When have you felt the Spirit remind you of your divine heritage?

Q: Think about the things you do every day. In what specific ways can you keep your divine identity at the center of everything you do?

_____

_____

_____

_____

_____

_____

_____

_____

_____

Q: How can you be better at seeing and honoring the divinity in others, especially those with whom you may disagree?

_____

_____

_____

_____

_____

_____

_____

_____

_____

_____

_____

_____

Your Divine Identity

Study 2

DAILY READING:

"Knowing Who You Are—and Who You Have Always Been," by Sheri Dew
BYU Women's Conference 2001

Abraham 3:22–23 • Doctrine and Covenants 138:55

Q: Sister Dew refers to the attributes of being "noble and great, courageous and determined, faithful and fearless." How can understanding and honoring your divine identity help you grow more deeply into each of those attributes?

_____

_____

_____

_____

_____

_____

_____

_____

_____

_____

_____

_____

_____

_____

_____

_____

_____

Q: What does it mean to you to be "among the noble and great ones" and to be "of noble birthright"?

_____

_____

_____

_____

_____

_____

_____

_____

_____

Q: How does Satan distort your understanding and perception of who you really are? What tactics does he use on you specifically, that make the "natural man" surface? How can you combat those tactics and live more consistently and fully in your true, divine identity?

_____

_____

_____

_____

_____

_____

_____

_____

_____

_____

Your Divine Identity

Study 3

DAILY READING:

"Remember Who You Are!" by Elaine S. Dalton
April 2010 General Conference

Joshua 3:5 • Alma 5:14

Q: Sister Dalton references Joshua 3:5, which says to "sanctify yourselves: for tomorrow the Lord will do wonders among you." In what ways can you sanctify yourself to honor your divine identity and become who you were created to be?

_____

_____

_____

_____

_____

_____

_____

_____

_____

_____

_____

_____

_____

_____

_____

_____

Q: The messages of the world are growing ever louder, seeking to "dismay, discourage, distract, delay, and disqualify" us. The Holy Ghost whispers the opposite. How can we create quiet space to hear the Spirit so we can live "in the world" but not be "of the world"?

Q: We are God's children—His very offspring! What does it mean to receive "His image in your countenance"? How can we live so that others will see Him in us?

Your Divine Identity

Study 4

DAILY READING:

"Am I a Child of God?" by Brian K. Taylor
April 2018 General Conference

Genesis 1:26 • Moses 1:4, 6, 12–13

Q: Genesis 1:26 tells us that we were each created in the image of God. In what ways do you resemble your heavenly parents physically? In what ways are you like your heavenly parents spiritually?

_____

_____

_____

_____

_____

_____

_____

_____

_____

_____

_____

_____

_____

_____

_____

_____

_____

_____

_____

Q: How can understanding our own divine identity and teaching others (including children) about their divine identity help when trials and challenges come?

_____

_____

_____

_____

_____

_____

_____

_____

_____

_____

Q: The words we tell ourselves are powerful. We believe what we think. What truths and positive affirmations can you recite daily to believe more in your divine identity as a child of God?

_____

_____

_____

_____

_____

_____

_____

_____

_____

_____

Your Divine Identity

Study 5

DAILY READING:

"Discovering the Divinity Within,"
by Rosemary M. Wixom
October 2015 General Conference

Job 33:4 • "The Family: A Proclamation to the World" • 2 Peter 1:4

Q: Because of our divine nature, we're drawn to service. How are you inclined to serve others? Who have you been prepared to serve?

_____

_____

_____

_____

Q: Because of our divine nature, we are made to learn and gain knowledge. What interests you? What would you like to know more about? Write those things down. Your interests toward certain subjects are a good indication of what God wants you to learn more about.

_____

_____

_____

_____

Invitation:

Spend a few minutes today in prayer, asking Heavenly Father who needs you and how. Listen for the answer, then go and do.

Notes

The *worth* of a soul is its capacity to *become* as *God.* —Thomas S. Monson

Week Two

Your Divine Worth

As a child of God, you are divine! Your worth can't be measured monetarily. In fact, Brigham Young taught, "The least, the most inferior spirit now upon the earth . . . is worth worlds" ("Remarks").

The world measures the worth of a person based on status, financial investments, beauty, rank, clothing size, and other superficial standards. Those things will not last—not one of them will be taken with us when we die. This way of judging value is not God's way. "God is your Father. He loves you. He and your Mother in Heaven value you beyond any measure. You are unique. One of a kind, made of the eternal intelligence which gives you claim upon eternal life. Let there be no question in your mind about your value as an individual. The whole intent of the gospel plan is to provide an opportunity for each of you to reach your fullest potential, which is eternal progression and the possibility of godhood" (Spencer W. Kimball, "Privileges and Responsibilities of Sisters").

Perhaps the most appropriate quote I've found on the subject is this: "The worth of a soul is its capacity to become as God" (Thomas S. Monson, "Our Sacred Priesthood Trust"). How wonderful and valuable and important you are!

Memorization Scripture:

Proverbs 3:15

"She is more precious than rubies: and all the things
thou canst desire are not to be compared unto her."

Personal Affirmation:

As a child of God, I have an inherent worth that is far more valuable than
looks, wealth, or status. I am priceless, and my heavenly parents love me
beyond measure.

Your Divine Worth

DAILY READING:

"Value beyond Measure," by Joy D. Jones
October 2017 General Conference

Doctrine and Covenants 18:10–11
Doctrine and Covenants 121:45–46

Q: Doctrine and Covenants 18:11 reminds us of the great and unimaginable sacrifice that the Savior made for each one of us individually. How does this verse remind you of your divine worth?

_____

_____

_____

_____

_____

_____

Q: How does your confidence in your divine worth and purpose grow as you fill your heart and mind with charity and virtue? (Doctrine and Covenants 121:45–46)

_____

_____

_____

_____

_____

Q: What is the difference between "worth" and "worthiness"? How can you recognize where you are in both of those areas?

_____

_____

_____

_____

_____

_____

_____

_____

_____

_____

Q: What can you do when negative thoughts creep in and seek to destroy your perception of your divine worth?

_____

_____

_____

_____

_____

_____

_____

_____

_____

_____

Your Divine Worth

Study 2

DAILY READING:

"Our Divinely Based Worth," by Barbara Day Lockhart
June 1995 *Ensign*

1 Samuel 16:7 • Doctrine and Covenants 88:15 • 2 Nephi 31:19

Q: Read Doctrine and Covenants 88:15. How does the fact that our Father in Heaven gave each of us a magnificent body to house our spirits confirm the great value He places on you?

_____

_____

_____

_____

_____

_____

_____

_____

_____

_____

_____

_____

_____

_____

_____

_____

_____

_____

Q: What does the world tell you is valuable? What does the Lord tell you is valuable?

_____

_____

_____

_____

_____

_____

_____

_____

Q: In what ways does "relying wholly upon the merits of him who is mighty to save" (2 Nephi 31:19) help you recognize your own worth and the worth of others?

_____

_____

_____

_____

_____

_____

_____

_____

_____

Your Divine Worth

Study 3

DAILY READING:

"Gift of Worth: Acts of Worthiness," by Barbara Day Lockhart
BYU Women's Conference May 2006

Jacob 2:21 • Matthew 22:36–39

Q: Read Matthew 22:36–39. The two great commandments are well known: "Love the Lord thy God with all thy heart, soul and mind" and "Love thy neighbour as thyself." Many of us think that the phrase "love thy neighbor as thyself" means we need to be more loving toward our neighbor, yet we often treat our neighbors better than we treat ourselves. Perhaps this phrase could mean that we need to value our own personal worth more and be as kind to ourselves as we are to others. How can you show yourself more love and respect?

_____

_____

_____

_____

_____

_____

_____

_____

_____

_____

_____

Q: Sister Lockhart talks about the value of our physical body. What can you do to show more respect for your body? How can you show more love and appreciation for the body that our heavenly parents have created specifically for you?

_____

_____

_____

_____

_____

_____

_____

Q: Think about Sister Lockhart's question and answer it for yourself: "What does knowing that we are literal children of God—that our whole soul, body and spirit, is sacred and that we are precious to Him just as we are—what does this do for our lives?"

_____

_____

_____

_____

_____

_____

_____

_____

_____

Your Divine Worth

Study 4

DAILY READING:

"You Matter to Him," by Dieter F. Uchtdorf
October 2011 General Conference

Moses 1:38–39 • Mosiah 3:19

Q: Think of the paradox referred to in President Uchtdorf's talk—Satan appeals to the natural man by using flattery and increasing pride. But the Lord teaches us to be humble and meek, submissive and patient. These are all characteristics that Satan will tell you are weaknesses, but these are the very things that the Lord values. How can you recognize and turn away from pride in order to cultivate childlike humility?

_____

_____

_____

_____

_____

_____

_____

_____

_____

_____

_____

_____

_____

Q: Moses 1:38–39 teaches that God's whole work, all of His glory, revolves around getting us back to live with Him for the eternities. What does this tell you about your value and worth to Him?

_____

_____

_____

_____

_____

_____

_____

_____

_____

_____

_____

_____

_____

_____

_____

_____

_____

_____

Invitation:

Satan loves to deceive through discouragement. There may be nothing he enjoys more than watching someone question their worth as a divine being. The next time a discouraging or self-defeating thought enters your mind, say aloud the words "I am a child of God" until that thought is replaced by the beautiful reminder of your inherent value.

Your Divine Worth

Study 5

DAILY READING:

"Am I Good Enough? Will I Make It?" by J. Devn Cornish
October 2016 General Conference

Doctrine and Covenants 50:24 • Mosiah 26:29–30

Q: We know that we are children of God. Doctrine and Covenants 50:24 states, "That which is of God is light." If we receive this light and continue in Him, we will receive more light, growing "brighter and brighter." How can seeking to obtain light and "continuing in Him" reinforce our divine worth?

_____

_____

_____

_____

Q: Have you ever felt that mistakes you've made have diminished your worth? Have you ever felt shame in your weaknesses, thinking that God must not love you as much? Mosiah 26:29–30 says that when we sincerely repent and come unto Him, He will forgive us "as often as [we] repent." He values us above all else, and nothing we can ever do will diminish our worth in His sight. How can you work on a daily habit of repentance?

_____

_____

_____

_____

_____

Notes

Moses 6:56 – And it is given unto them to know *good from evil:* wherefore they are agents unto themselves, and I have given unto you another law and commandment.

Week Three

Your Divine Agency

We are divine beings with a divine heritage and destiny. However, the world will discredit these truths and try to distort our perspective by telling us what we aren't and what we need to be. When we give into these worldly views, we allow Satan into our minds, distorting our vision and muddying truth. It is imperative that we retain an eternal perspective and maintain our connection to the Spirit at all times. As we use our divine gift of agency every day, we must remember who we truly are. By holding tightly to the truth of our divine nature, we will be able to see more clearly and make the choices that will keep us progressing toward eternal life.

"As the developments of technology and communication ever press the modern world upon us, being in the world but not of the world requires that we make constant choices and decisions (see John 17:14). Spiritual discernment is paramount. As disciples of Christ, we must make the gift of the Holy Ghost a conscious, daily, prayerful part of our lives. How can we use this heavenly gift as a vital compass for our daily actions? We must believe that even in our weaknesses, the still, small voice we feel comes from our Father. We must pray and ask and seek and then not be afraid when answers come into our heart and mind. Believe they are divine. They are" (Neil L. Andersen, "A Gift Worthy of Added Care").

Memorization Scripture:

2 Nephi 2:26

"And the Messiah cometh in the fulness of time, that he may redeem the children of men from the fall. And because that they are redeemed from the fall they have become free forever, knowing good from evil; to act for themselves and not to be acted upon . . ."

Personal Affirmation:

God loves and trusts me enough to allow me to make my own choices.
I have been taught and my heart knows what is right.
I choose goodness. I choose love. I choose joy. I choose Jesus Christ.

Your Divine Agency

Study 1

DAILY READING:

"'Choose You This Day': Using Our Agency to Arise as Women of God," by Sharon G. Larsen
BYU Women's Conference 2000

Helaman 14:30 • 2 Nephi 2:11

Q: God created opposition in all things. Opposites are a divine part of His plan for us: light and darkness, earth and sea, warmth and cold, right and wrong. How can the opposition in your life lead you to create a deeper relationship with Heavenly Father?

_____

_____

_____

_____

Q: Think about this quote by Elder L. Tom Perry: "It was no small thing for Satan to disregard man's agency. In fact, it became the principal issue over which the War in Heaven was fought. Victory in the War in Heaven was a victory for [our] agency" ("Obedience to Law Is Liberty"). As a spiritual being, you fought in that war for Christ's plan! How does knowing that help you understand the importance of honoring your agency? Does it change the way you think about how you make decisions?

_____

_____

_____

Your Divine Agency

Study 2

DAILY READING:

"Free Forever, to Act for Themselves," by D. Todd Christofferson
October 2014 General Conference

Moses 6:56 • Moses 4:3–4

Q: Read Moses 4:3–4. We learn that Satan's game plan, his mightiest tactic, was to destroy the agency of man. He didn't attempt to attack families, he didn't seek to destroy faith—he was simply determined to take away our ability to choose. What does that tell you about how important and valuable agency is? How can you respect your personal gift to choose as you make decisions for your life?

_____

_____

_____

Q: Elder Christofferson speaks of justice, mercy, and repentance. He states, "By making repentance a condition for receiving the gift of grace, God enables us to retain responsibility for ourselves. Repentance respects and sustains our moral agency." What connections can you make between agency and repentance? How does knowing repentance is a choice change how you feel about it?

_____

_____

_____

_____

Your Divine Agency

Study 3

DAILY READING:

"The Freedom to Become," by Dieter F. Uchtdorf
BYU–Idaho Devotional March 2020

Matthew 6:19–21 • Genesis 6:8, 22 • 2 Nephi 10:23

Q: We read in Genesis 6 about the great wickedness that flooded the earth—probably not much different than the wickedness we see today. This grieved the Lord, and He could see that the thoughts of men's hearts were "evil continually." Because Noah was just and walked with God, he "found grace in the eyes of the Lord." What does acceptance mean by the world's standards? How does this acceptance differ from the grace we seek in the eyes of the Lord? What can you change in your life that will take you from being accepted by the world to finding grace in the eyes of the Lord?

_____

_____

_____

_____

_____

_____

_____

_____

_____

_____

Q: Elder Uchtdorf says, "You, also, have the priceless blessing to choose who you wish to become. Just know that every choice brings with it its own set of constraints, restrictions, and consequences." In 2 Nephi 10:23 it speaks of the divine gift to act for ourselves but reminds us that we're not free to choose the consequences of our actions. Who do you want to become? What sacrifices are you willing to live with to become the person you want to be?

Your Divine Agency

Study 4

DAILY READING:

"The Gift of Agency," by Wolfgang H. Paul
April 2006 General Conference

Abraham 3:25 • Moses 4:2

Q: Read Abraham 3:25. This life is a time for our agency to be tested. Elder
Paul says, "If we did not have this wonderful gift of agency, we would
not be able to show our Father in Heaven whether we will do all that He
commanded us. I have learned that as we obey our Heavenly Father's commandments, our faith increases, we grow in wisdom and spiritual strength,
and it becomes easier for us to make right choices." Have you found this to
be true in your life? If so, how?

_____

_____

_____

_____

_____

_____

_____

_____

_____

_____

_____

_____

Q: Moses 4:2 reminds us that Christ sided with the Father's plan of agency and redemption. Elder Paul recounts seeing a bumper sticker that said, "I do what I want." He then says, "We should make our choices using the same criteria [as the Savior did in Moses 4:2]. Instead of saying, 'I do what I want,' our motto should be 'I do what the Father wants me to do.'" Think critically about your life right now. What do you want? Do your desires match the Lord's desires for you? How can you shift your desires to be more in line with His? What insight comes to you as you ponder these questions?

_____

_____

_____

_____

_____

_____

_____

_____

_____

_____

_____

_____

_____

_____

_____

_____

_____

_____

_____

Your Divine Agency

Study 5

DAILY READING:

"Our Essential Spiritual Agency," by Robert D. Hales
BYU Speeches September 2010

2 Nephi 2:26–27 • 2 Nephi 28:8 • John 14:15

Q: Elder Hales says, "Whenever we use our agency, we are either choosing to move toward a new door with many possibilities or into a closed corner with very few options." Have there been times in your life that your agency has been diminished because of a choice that you made? How can you avoid this trap?

_____

_____

_____

_____

_____

Q: No matter your age or circumstances, the Lord has an important work for you to do. Do you know what it is? If not, seek counsel from Him. Once you know, how can you use your divine gift of agency to perform the work He has for you?

_____

_____

_____

_____

_____

Notes

Doctrine and Covenants 46:8 – Wherefore, beware . . . that ye may not be deceived, seek ye earnestly the best gifts, always remembering for what they are given;

Your Divine Gifts

Divine gifts are within each of us. Not one person was sent to earth without something that is inherently easy for them. Perhaps you are musical or eloquent or an amazing teacher. Or maybe you possess the gift of kindness or forgiveness or a believing heart.

President George Q. Cannon said, "Every man and woman in the Church of Christ can have the gifts of the Spirit of God divided to them according to their faith and as God wills. . . . How many of you . . . are seeking for these gifts that God has promised to bestow? . . . If any of us are imperfect, it is our duty to pray for the gift that will make us perfect. Have I imperfections? I am full of them. What is my duty? To pray to God to give me the gifts that will correct [my] imperfections. If I am an angry man, it is my duty to pray for charity, which suffereth long and is kind. . . . God has promised to give the gifts that are necessary for [our] perfection" ("Seeking Spiritual Gifts").

Some spiritual gifts are easily seen by others. Some spiritual gifts are not. It's easy to look at others' talents and abilities and compare them to our own: "I wish I could sing like her" or "I wish I could teach that way." Let us remember that the greatest attributes of the Savior were quiet. Let us seek to develop those things in ourselves that will help us be more like Him.

Memorization Scripture:

Doctrine and Covenants 6:10

"Behold thou hast a gift, and blessed art thou because of thy gift. Remember it is sacred and cometh from above."

Personal Affirmation:

I am unique and have been sent to earth with special, personal gifts from my heavenly parents. These traits and talents enrich my life, help me grow, and enable me to bless the lives of those around me.

Your Divine Gifts

DAILY READING:

"Spiritual Gifts," by Peggy S. Worthen
BYU Speeches January 2019

Doctrine and Covenants 46:12, 26

Q: Read Doctrine and Covenants 46:12, 26. In what ways can you honor and appreciate the gifts of others? How can you share your own gifts with others? And how can you avoid the trap of comparing your gifts to theirs?

_____

_____

_____

_____

_____

_____

_____

_____

_____

_____

_____

_____

_____

_____

_____

_____

_____

_____

Q: Sister Worthen refers to an *Ensign* article by Elder Marvin J. Ashton in which he says, "Taken at random, let me mention a few gifts that are not always evident . . . but that are very important: the gift of asking; the gift of listening; the gift of hearing and using a still, small voice; the gift of being able to weep; the gift of avoiding contention; the gift of being agreeable; the gift of avoiding vain repetition; the gift of seeking that which is righteous; the gift of not passing judgment; the gift of looking to God for guidance; the gift of being a disciple; the gift of caring for others; the gift of being able to ponder; the gift of offering prayer; the gift of bearing a mighty testimony; and the gift of receiving the Holy Ghost." In reading that list of less conspicuous gifts, did you note any that you have? How can you develop the ones you may not possess but would like to?

Your Divine Gifts

Study 2

DAILY READING:

"Finding Your Purpose," by Julianne H. Grose
BYU Speeches May 2019

Alma 32:41–43

Q: Sister Grose mentions three situations where the Lord "moved mountains" for her students to be able to use their gifts in the world of science and research. Have you seen the Lord move mountains in your life in order for you to be able to develop or use your gifts? How has this blessed your life? How has it blessed the lives of others?

_____

_____

_____

_____

_____

_____

_____

_____

_____

_____

_____

_____

_____

_____

Q: Sister Grose reminds us that the whole purpose of this earth life is for us to gain experience, acquire knowledge, and make choices. Our heavenly parents want us to succeed and be our best selves. The Savior believes in us; He atoned for each of us, allowing us to change and become better. It is part of the plan to develop talents and gifts. Are there things in your life you'd like to accomplish or learn to do? Do you have interests that you're drawn to time and time again? Having an idea or desire surface over and over is a good indication that this is something the Lord wants you to pursue.

_____

_____

_____

_____

_____

_____

_____

_____

_____

_____

_____

_____

_____

_____

_____

_____

_____

Invitation:

Even the most talented and gifted among us has new things to learn and skills to develop. Read Alma 32:41–43 and ponder the ways you can start to develop new gifts. Ask God to help you recognize the areas in which He needs you to excel.

Your Divine Gifts

Study 3

DAILY READING:

"I Have a Work for Thee," by John C. Pingree Jr.
October 2017 General Conference

Ephesians 2:10 • Doctrine and Covenants 58:27–28
Doctrine and Covenants 11:8 • Mosiah 23:10

Q: Elder Pingree refers to Mosiah 23:10 and teaches that some of our gifts will surface in times of difficulty or trials. Have you noticed strengths that you've acquired in enduring hard things? How can you be more appreciative of difficulty?

_____

_____

_____

_____

_____

_____

_____

_____

_____

_____

_____

_____

_____

Q: Elder Pingree reminds us in this beautiful talk that we are who the Lord needs right now. It is the ordinary among us who will do great things and help prepare the world for the Second Coming of the Savior. He quotes President Nelson as saying, "The Lord needs you to change the world. As you accept and follow His will for you, you will find yourself accomplishing the impossible!" What are specific ways in which you can use your unique gifts, however small they may be, to "change the world"?

Invitation:

Take time in your personal prayers to thank our Heavenly Father for the many spiritual gifts, big and small, with which He's blessed you.

Your Divine Gifts

Study 4

DAILY READING:

"How Vast Is Our Purpose," by Jean B. Bingham
BYU Women's Conference 2017

1 Corinthians 2:9 • Mosiah 4:9

Q: Each of us feels "ordinary" sometimes. Each of us feels underqualified or not quite good enough at something. However, our heavenly parents see the potential we have and know our strengths. To echo Sister Bingham's question, what do you want to accomplish in your life? What are your goals and aspirations? These things will lead you to recognize previously unrecognized gifts you can develop. Write them down and start setting goals.

_____

_____

_____

_____

Q: Read Mosiah 4:9. Think carefully about your life. What has God created in you that will help you be successful and fulfill the purpose you've been put on earth to accomplish?

_____

_____

_____

_____

_____

Your Divine Gifts

Study 5

DAILY READING:

"Discover, Honor, and Develop Your Gifts," by Elizabeth Ricks
BYU Women's Conference 2008

Doctrine and Covenants 46:7–8,11 • Moroni 10:8–18
Your Patriarchal Blessing

Q: Sister Ricks reviews the parable of the talents. Are there talents that you hide for one reason or another? Are you embarrassed to let certain gifts be used and seen? Do you hide certain God-given abilities because you don't want to be viewed as prideful? Consider how you can humbly and confidently use the spiritual gifts you've been given to bless others' lives.

_____

_____

_____

_____

_____

_____

_____

_____

_____

Invitation:

Read your patriarchal blessing with a notepad on hand. As you read, look for mentions of small or hidden spiritual gifts that you may not have paid attention to before. Write them down and pray about how to develop them.

1 Peter 2:21 – For even hereunto *were ye called:* because Christ also suffered for us, leaving us an example, that ye should *follow his steps:*

Week Five

Your Divine Potential

The Lord revealed our identity and potential when He said, "Behold . . . thou art an elect lady, whom I have called." He has admonished each of us to "walk the paths of virtue". We are daughters of God. We are noble and even elect. We will never be able to live as women of God if we let the world define what that means. We have a great work to do.

"We really must individually come to understand who we are, the potential we have, and the incredible trust we have been given by our Father in Heaven to be here on the earth now in this Last Dispensation of the Fullness of Times. Just as Esther came to understand her identity and mission, we must do the same. 'Who knoweth whether thou art come to the Kingdom for such a time as this?'

"This is why the injunction is given to us in the Doctrine and Covenants to 'arise and shine forth that thy light may be a standard for the nations.' We have come to the kingdom for such a time as this! We can energetically lead the world in everything that is virtuous, praiseworthy and of good report—a return to virtue and to moral strength and character. As Eliza R. Snow said to the women of her day, I repeat today—'It is not for you to be led by the women of the world; it is for you to lead . . . the women of the world, in everything that is . . . purifying to the children of men.' As daughters of God, we were born to lead" (Elaine S. Dalton, "Arise and Shine Forth: A Return to Virtue").

Memorization Scripture:

3 Nephi 27:27

"Therefore, what manner of men ought ye to be?
Verily I say unto you, even as I am."

Personal Affirmation:

I am a divine child of God, and therefore, I have within me all of the spiritual DNA that I need to grow to be like my heavenly parents. They have blessed me with all I need to become like them.

Your Divine Potential

Study 1

DAILY READING:

"Keys to Progress: An Eternal Perspective," by Jean B. Bingham
BYU–Idaho Devotional November 2018

1 Peter 5:10 • Jeremiah 29:12–13

Q: 1 Peter 5:10 reminds us that suffering is a part of this life. We know that because of Jesus Christ, all suffering will eventually end; but when we're in the middle of a trial, it can be difficult to trust that there's peace and happiness ahead. What fundamental truths can you lean on to endure trials with a hopeful, eternal perspective?

_____

_____

_____

_____

_____

_____

_____

_____

_____

_____

_____

_____

_____

_____

_____

Q: Echoing the question Sister Bingham poses in her talk, ask yourself, "What can I do in my [current] situation to become all that my heavenly parents have designed me to be?"

Q: Personal prayer, scripture study, and temple worship are three regular practices we can establish that consistently remind us of our divine potential. Looking at your life right now, in what ways can you deepen your experiences with the Divine through these practices?

Your Divine Potential

Study 2

DAILY READING:

"Becoming Women of God," by Mary N. Cook
BYU Women's Conference April 2011

Mosiah 18:9 • 2 Nephi 9:39

Q: In her talk, Sister Cook stresses remembering at all times exactly who we are. She warns against Satan's aggressive efforts to distract us from the truth of our divine nature. Are your daily desires, priorities, and actions consistent with your identity as a daughter of God?

_____

_____

_____

_____

_____

_____

_____

_____

_____

_____

_____

_____

_____

_____

_____

_____

_____

Q: Part of living up to your potential as a divine daughter of God means serving as an example for others to follow. Who looks to you as an example? Daughters and sons? Students? Youth in the church? What messages are you sending to them about who they are as they watch you live your life?

_____

_____

_____

_____

_____

_____

_____

_____

_____

_____

_____

_____

_____

_____

_____

_____

_____

_____

_____

_____

Invitation:

Create space in your day, even just ten or fifteen minutes, for stillness and silence. Sit and listen for promptings and impressions with an open heart and an open mind. The Lord will whisper to you the essential, personal things that you need to know and do to achieve your divine potential.

Your Divine Potential

Study 3

DAILY READING:

"Becoming a Work of Art," by Ulisses Soares
BYU Speeches November 2013

1 Nephi 15:24 • 1 Nephi 8:5–34

Q: Michelangelo used a hammer and chisel to create out of solid marble his masterpiece the Pietà. In like manner, God is making something magnificent out of our lives. In what ways can you feel Him shaping your life? Is He knocking off edges here and making small ruts there? How is He polishing you?

_____

_____

_____

_____

_____

_____

_____

_____

_____

_____

_____

_____

_____

_____

_____

Q: Elder Soares discusses temptation and how it endangers our progression. Think honestly about your life. What temptations do you face? How can you eliminate those things that will inevitably harm or distract you and keep you from remembering your purpose and potential?

Q: Why are you on earth at this time in history? You have a marvelous work to do. The adversary works day and night to distract us from remembering our divine potential. What comes to mind as you think of ways to eliminate distractions and keep your eyes locked on the Savior and the potential He sees in you?

Your Divine Potential

Study 4

DAILY READING:

"Eternal Perspective and Our Potential," by Euleza Hymas
BYU–Idaho Devotional September 2015

Proverbs 9:9–10 • 2 Nephi 31:20

Q: Sister Hymas says, "In order for us to meet our full potential, we are expected to gain knowledge, observe, and learn." In what ways can you work toward your full potential by learning, observing, and gaining knowledge? How do you learn best?

_____

_____

_____

_____

_____

Q: Each of us will experience setbacks, roadblocks, and hardships on our journey. What can you do to maintain an eternal perspective and remember your divine potential as you face these difficulties?

_____

_____

_____

_____

_____

Your Divine Potential

Study 5

DAILY READING:

"Covenant Women in Partnership with God,"
by Henry B. Eyring
October 2019 General Conference

Moses 1:39 • Doctrine and Covenants 14:7

Q: Read Moses 1:39. God's glory is to bring to pass our eternal life. President Eyring quotes President Nelson who said, "To help another human being reach one's celestial potential is part of the divine mission of woman." Thus, when we help others in their journey back to our heavenly parents, we are acting as they act. Who have you been called to help? How can you be an instrument in the Lord's hands as you aid others in discovering their divine potential?

_____

_____

_____

_____

_____

Q: Doctrine and Covenants 14:7 states, "If you keep my commandments and endure to the end you shall have eternal life." The covenants we make with God to obey and endure create a partnership full of power and purpose. How could being more obedient strengthen your partnership with God?

_____

_____

_____

_____

John 17:3 – And this is *life eternal*, that they might know thee the *only true God*, and *Jesus Christ*, whom thou hast sent.

Your Divine Destiny

Your divine destiny is to become like God. It is to gain all that our heavenly parents have: all light, all knowledge, all power, all love. They created you for this very purpose. You are brave and faithful and valiant and chose to follow their plan. You are one of the chosen spirits saved to come to earth at this specific time.

Sheri Dew described it this way: "It's akin to being chosen to run the last leg of a relay, where the coach always positions his strongest runner. You were recommended to help run the last leg of the relay that began with Adam and Eve because your premortal spiritual valor indicated you would have the courage and the determination to face the world at its worst, to do combat with the evil one during his heyday, and, in spite of it all, to be fearless in building the kingdom of God. You simply must understand this, because you were born to lead by virtue of who you are, the covenants you have made, and the fact that you are here now in the 11th hour" ("You Were Born To Lead, You Were Born for Glory").

Our heavenly parents know you well and saved you for now because of the mighty work they have for you to do—in your families, in your communities, in your congregations, and in your own personal life. You are an essential piece of their plan. Turn to them and to the Savior. Trust them. They will help you fulfill your mission and return home to them.

Memorization Scripture:

Doctrine & Covenants 132:19–20

"Ye . . . shall inherit thrones, kingdoms, principalities, and powers, dominions, all heights and depths. . . . Then shall they be gods, because they have no end; therefore shall they be from everlasting to everlasting, because they continue; then shall they be above all, because all things are subject undo them."

Personal Affirmation:

As a child of God, I am an heir to all He has. I look forward with faith to eternal life and celestial glory: endless joy, endless knowledge, and endless love.

Your Divine Destiny

Study 1

DAILY READING:

"Desire," by Dallin H. Oaks
April 2011 General Conference

Enos 1:12 • Alma 22:16

Q: Read Enos 1:12 and Alma 22:16. These scriptures teach us that having desires is important. Personal desires go hand in hand with our agency. For many people, there is a struggle between having desires and being greedy. But Heavenly Father wants to give us the desires of our hearts in the same way that we want to give our children the things that they want for Christmas—not just the things we think they should have. What desires do you have? How can you adjust your desires to give "highest priority to the things of eternity"?

_____

_____

_____

_____

_____

_____

_____

_____

_____

_____

_____

_____

_____

Q: "Desires dictate our priorities, priorities shape our choices, and choices determine our actions. The desires we act on determine our changing, our achieving, and our becoming." This pattern of creation laid out by President Oaks takes us from desiring to becoming. What are your daily desires? What are your eternal desires? How can you create goals based on those desires that help you achieve your divine destiny?

Your Divine Destiny

Study 2

DAILY READING:

"Your Eternal Identity and Destiny," by Brian Tonks
BYU–Idaho Devotional December 2016

Moses 1 • Abraham 3:24–28

Q: You are a unique and beloved child of God, and He has a sacred work specifically for you to do. Have you heard that call? Do you know what your unique purpose is? It is in discovering, and then fulfilling this purpose that you will begin to discover your divine destiny. Ask, seek, listen. Then record what He tells you He needs you to do.

_____

_____

_____

_____

_____

_____

_____

_____

_____

_____

_____

_____

_____

_____

Q: Satan is very good at distorting our divine identities. He uses different tactics on different people. What are some of the triggers that Satan uses to cause you to doubt your true identity and live in your false identity (the natural man)? In what ways can you counter those thoughts when they enter your mind?

_____

_____

_____

_____

_____

_____

_____

_____

Q: Our divine destiny is to become as God is. This is quite the loaded statement. What does that mean for you? What can you do each day to remember who you are and what is meant for you?

_____

_____

_____

_____

_____

_____

_____

_____

Your Divine Destiny

Study 3

DAILY READING:

"Salvation and Exaltation," by Russell M. Nelson
April 2008 General Conference

2 Nephi 31:20 • Doctrine and Covenants 68:28 • Alma 12:24

Q: Read 2 Nephi 31:20. We know that obtaining eternal life is the divine destiny of all who follow the Savior and endure to the end. How does focusing on and following the Savior make your life simpler/happier/easier? How does following the Savior lead us to our divine destiny?

_____

_____

_____

_____

_____

_____

_____

_____

_____

_____

_____

_____

_____

_____

_____

_____

Q: Just as on an airplane, where adults are instructed to secure their oxygen masks before assisting others, we cannot influence others to believe in Christ or live His gospel unless we have done those things ourselves. What specific things do you need to do to strengthen your testimony so you can help strengthen others?

_____

_____

_____

_____

_____

_____

_____

Q: Read Alma 12:24. This is our preparatory state! What will you do today to prepare to meet God?

_____

_____

_____

_____

_____

_____

_____

_____

_____

_____

Your Divine Destiny

Study 4

DAILY READING:

"You Were Born to Lead, You Were Born for Glory,"
by Sheri Dew
BYU Speeches December 2003

1 Peter 2:9 • Isaiah 62:2–3 • 1 Nephi 14:14

Q: Sister Dew compares us to the strong runners chosen to run the last leg of a relay race. You were reserved for this day because of your courage, strength, and faithfulness. He trusts you and He needs you. You were born to lead. In what ways can you be a leader to those around you—your family, your friends and associates, and even strangers?

_____

_____

_____

_____

_____

_____

_____

_____

_____

_____

_____

_____

_____

_____

_____

_____

Q: Read 1 Nephi 14:14. Part of our divine destiny involves understanding, seeking for, and appropriately using the power of God. What is the power of God? It is the priesthood. All of God's faithful, covenant children—men and women—on the earth today have access to this priesthood power. It is essential that we understand what this means for us. In what ways can you access divine priesthood power in your life?

_____

_____

_____

_____

_____

_____

_____

_____

Q: Sister Dew makes this great observation: "There is only one thing the power of God and the power of Satan have in common: Neither can influence us unless we allow them to." How will you determine to increase God's influence in your life? How will you determine to decrease the power Satan has in your life?

_____

_____

_____

_____

_____

_____

_____

Your Divine Destiny

DAILY READING:

"Our Identity and Our Destiny," by Tad R. Callister
BYU Speeches August 2012

Genesis 3:22 • Psalm 82:6
Doctrine and Covenants 132:20 • 3 Nephi 27:27

Q: Review Psalm 82:6 and Doctrine and Covenants 132:20. When we understand our divine destiny to become as God is, we recognize this potential in all His children. How can we start to view others, especially those with whom we may disagree, as potential heirs of God?

_____

_____

_____

_____

_____

_____

_____

_____

_____

_____

_____

_____

_____

_____

_____

Q: Elder Callister lays out a substantial spiritual, as well as logical, argument about mankind's potential to become like God. That is our destiny. He poses an important question for each of us to answer: Why is it so critical to have a correct vision of this divine destiny of godliness, of which the scriptures and other witnesses so clearly testify?

_____

_____

_____

_____

_____

_____

_____

_____

_____

_____

_____

_____

_____

_____

_____

_____

_____

Invitation:

Set aside time to write the thoughts of your heart concerning your own divine identity and worth and the choices you'll commit to making. Write about your spiritual gifts, your divine potential, and the divine destiny that is waiting for you. Read it routinely. Add to it. Never forget the divinity that is within you.

Reflect and Review

1. How have you been able to see aspects of your heavenly parents in yourself as you've studied about your divine identity? In what ways can you keep the reminder of who you really are fresh in your mind each day?

_____

_____

_____

_____

_____

2. As you've read and pondered about your own divine worth, where have you seen yourself lacking in feelings of self-worth? How can you change that narrative and learn to both humbly and confidently own who you truly are and embrace your priceless nature?

_____

_____

_____

_____

_____

3. We believe that the gift of agency is one of the grandest gifts that heavenly parents have given their children. How has focusing on this aspect of the plan of happiness changed the way you view your ability to make choices? How has your perspective shifted in terms of allowing others to use that gift of agency freely?

_____

_____

_____

_____

_____

4. What have you learned about the divine gifts you've been given as you've worked through this book? Are there spiritual gifts that you don't yet have but that you desire? What goals can you establish to help this gift come to fruition? How can you include the Lord in your quest?

_____

_____

_____

_____

_____

5. In studying your divine potential—the God-given abilities that you've been given to become—how have you received confidence in yourself? How can you confidently move forward with new goals to propel you toward success in the ways you desire to grow and change?

_____

_____

_____

_____

_____

6. Your divine destiny is to become as God is and to inherit all that our heavenly parents have in store for you. How has studying this aspect of your divine identity allowed you to see things with a more eternal perspective? How can you maintain that eternal perspective as you move forward in this mortal life with the inevitable trials and challenges that will come?

_____

_____

_____

_____

_____

_____

References

Andersen, Neil L. "A Gift Worthy of Added Care." *Ensign*, The Church of Jesus Christ of Latter-Day Saints, Salt Lake City, UT, December 2010.

Ballard, M. Russell. "Children of Heavenly Father." BYU Speeches, 3 March 2020. https://speeches.byu.edu/talks/m-russell-ballard/children-heavenly-father/

Bingham, Jean B. "How Vast Is Our Purpose." BYU Women's Conference, 5 May 2017. https://www.churchofjesuschrist.org/callings/relief-society/messages-from-leaders/bingham-womens-conference-2017?lang=eng

—. "Keys to Progress: An Eternal Perspective." BYU–Idaho Devotionals, 27 November 2018. https://www.byui.edu/devotionals/sister-jean-b-bingham

Callister, Tad R. "Our Identity and Our Destiny." BYU Speeches, 14 August 2012. https://speeches.byu.edu/talks/tad-r-callister/our-identity-and-our-destiny/

Cannon, George Q. "Seeking Spiritual Gifts." *Ensign*, The Church of Jesus Christ of Latter-Day Saints, Salt Lake City, UT, April 2016.

Christofferson, D. Todd. "Free Forever, to Act for Themselves." *Ensign*, The Church of Jesus Christ of Latter-Day Saints, Salt Lake City, UT, November 2014.

Cook, Mary N. "Becoming Women of God." BYU Women's Conference, 28 April 2011. https://womensconference.byu.edu/sites/won1ensconference.ce.byu.edu/files/mary_n._cook_o.pdf

Cornish, J. Devn. "Am I Good Enough? Will I Make It?" *Ensign*, The Church of Jesus Christ of Latter-Day Saints, Salt Lake City, UT, November 2016.

Dalton, Elaine S. "Arise and Shine Forth: A Return to Virtue." BYU Women's Conference, 29 April 2010.

—. "Remember Who You Are!" *Ensign*, The Church of Jesus Christ of Latter-Day Saints, Salt Lake City, UT, May, 2010.

Dew, Sheri. "Knowing Who You Are—and Who You Have Always Been." BYU Women's Conference, 2001. https://womensconference.byu.edu/sites/womensconference.ce.byu.edu/files/dew_sheri_2. pdf

—. "You Were Born to Lead, You Were Born for Glory." BYU Speeches, 9 December 2003. https://speeches.byu.edu/talks/sheri-1-dew/born-lead-born-glory/

Eyring, Henry B. "Covenant Women in Partnership with God." *Ensign*, The Church of Jesus Christ of Latter-Day Saints, Salt Lake City, UT, November 2019.

Grose, Julianne H. "Finding Your Purpose." BYU Speeches, 21 May 2019. https://speeches.byu.edu/talks/julianne-h-grose/finding-your-purpose/

Hales, Robert D. "Agency: Our Essential Spiritual Gift." BYU Speeches, 14 September 2010. https://speeches.byu.edu/talks/robert-d-hales/our-essential-spiritual-agency/

Hymas, Euleza. "Eternal Perspective and Our Potential." BYU–Idaho Devotionals, 1 September 2015. https://www.byui.edu/devotionals/euleza-hymas

Jones, Joy D. "Value beyond Measure." *Ensign*, The Church of Jesus Christ of Latter-Day

Saints, Salt Lake City, UT, November 2017.

Kimball, Spencer W. "Privileges and Responsibilities of Sisters." *Ensign*, The Church of Jesus Christ of Latter-Day Saints, Salt Lake City, UT, November 1978.

Larsen, Sharon G. "Choose You This Day: Using Our Agency to Arise as Women of God." BYU Women's Conference, 2000. https://womensconference.byu.edu/sites/womens-conference.ce.byu.edu/files/larsen_sharon.pdf

Lockhart, Barbara Day. "Gifts of Worth: Acts of Worthiness." BYU Women's Conference, 4 May 2006. https://womensconference.byu.edu/sites/womensconference.ce.byu.edu/files/gift_of_worth-barbaradaylockhart.pdf

—. "Our Divinely Based Worth." Ensign, The Church of Jesus Christ of Latter-Day Saints, Salt Lake City, UT, June 1995.

Monson, Thomas S. "Our Sacred Priesthood Trust." *Ensign*, The Church of Jesus Christ of Latter-Day Saints, Salt Lake City, UT, May 2006.

Nelson, Russell M. "Salvation and Exaltation." *Ensign*, The Church of Jesus Christ of Latter-Day Saints, Salt Lake City, UT, May 2008.

Oaks, Dallin H. "Desire." *Ensign*, The Church of Jesus Christ of Latter-Day Saints, Salt Lake City, UT, May 2011.

Paul, Wolfgang H. "The Gift of Agency." *Ensign*, The Church of Jesus Christ of Latter-Day Saints, Salt Lake City, UT, May 2006.

Perry, L. Tom. "Obedience to Law Is Liberty." *Ensign*, The Church of Jesus Christ of Latter-Day Saints, Salt Lake City, UT, May 2013.

Pingree, John C., Jr. "I Have a Work for Thee." *Ensign*, The Church of Jesus Christ of Latter-Day Saints, Salt Lake City, UT, November 2017.

Ricks, Elizabeth. "Discover, Develop and Honor Your Gifts." BYU Women's Conference, 1 May 2008. https://womensconference.byu.edu/sites/womensconference.ce.byu.edu/files/elizabethricks2008.pdf

Soares, Ulisses S. "Becoming a Work of Art." BYU Speeches, 5 November 2013. https://speeches.byu.edu/talks/ulisses-soares/becoming-work-of-art/

Taylor, Brain K. "Am I a Child of God?" *Ensign*, The Church of Jesus Christ of Latter-Day Saints, Salt Lake City, UT, May 2018.

Tonks, Brian. "Your Eternal Identity and Destiny." BYU–Idaho Devotionals, 6 December 2016. https://www.byui.edu/devotionals/brian-tonks#transcript

Uchtdorf, Dieter F. "The Reflection in the Water." Church Educational System Fireside for young adults at Brigham Young University, 1 Nov. 2009.

—. "You Matter to Him." *Ensign*, The Church of Jesus Christ of Latter-Day Saints, Salt Lake City, UT, November 2011.

Uchtdorf, Dieter F. and Harriet R. "Freedom to Become," BYU–Idaho Devotionals, 1 March 2020. https://www.byui.edu/devotionals/elder-and-sister-dieter-f-uchtdorf

Wixom, Rosemary M. "Discovering the Divinity Within," *Ensign*, The Church of Jesus Christ of Latter-Day Saints, Salt Lake City, UT, November 2015.

Worthen, Peggy S. "Spiritual Gifts," BYU Speeches, 8 January 2019. https://speeches.byu.edu/talks/peggy-s-worthen/spiritual-gifts/

Young, Brigham. "Remarks," *Deseret News*, 6 March 1861, p. 2.

Seeking Diligently